Living Dinosaurs

Written and photographed by
Jonathan and Angela Scott

Contents

Collins

What are living dinosaurs?

Crocodiles and lizards have been living on Earth for millions of years. They were living at the same time as the dinosaurs. We know this because people have dug up their bones.

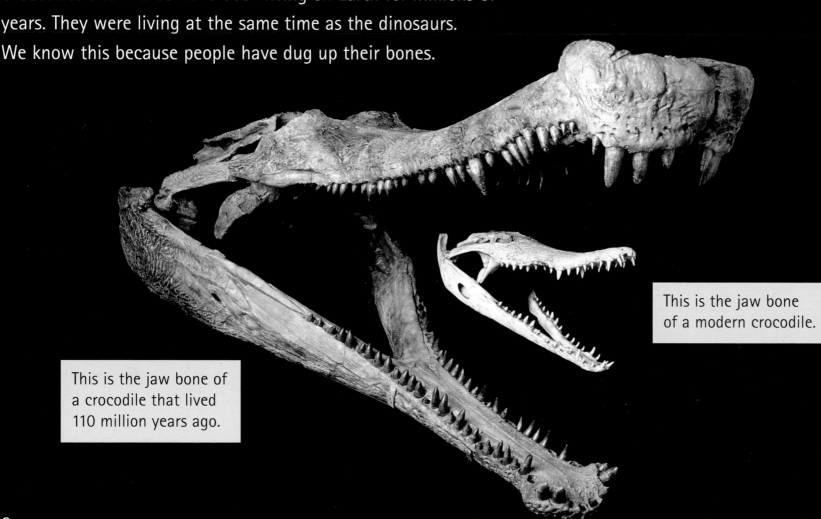

This is the jaw bone of a modern crocodile.

This is the jaw bone of a crocodile that lived 110 million years ago.

A Nile crocodile
chases its prey.

One of the reasons crocodiles and lizards have survived so long is
that they are good hunters and **scavengers**.

Crocodiles today

In Africa, herds of animals cross the River Mara each year, looking for fresh grass to eat. **Nile crocodiles** lie in wait for them.

Large crocodiles only need a few big meals a year. The rest of the time they mostly eat fish. Some crocodiles lie waiting for many months until an unlucky animal tries to cross the river.

Crocodiles are some of the best hunters in the world.
They are good at sneaking up on their **prey**.

Eyes, nostrils and ears are on top of their heads, so they can swim without being seen.

good hearing

good eyesight

good sense of smell

strong teeth for biting and tearing

a Nile crocodile

a saltwater crocodile
with its prey

Crocodiles grab their prey with their powerful jaws.
They can snap their jaws shut with enough power to crush a car door.

Crocodiles catch their prey and try to drown it by pulling it underwater. Crocodiles have a flap of skin to stop water going down their throats, so they can go underwater with their mouths open.

The throat flap is open.

8

A saltwater crocodile smashes its prey against the water, to break it into smaller pieces.

The throat flap is closed.

Crocodiles can grow up to seven metres long and live for up to 80 years.

Nile crocodiles have 66 to 68 teeth and if one gets broken, another grows in its place.

9

Weak points

Crocodiles have two weaknesses:

- They are powerful swimmers, but they have short legs and can only run short distances on land.

- Crocodiles can *shut* their jaws with great force. But they can't open them with the same power.

Crocodiles in danger

There are 23 different kinds of crocodile and alligator in the world today but some are in danger of dying out. This is because towns and cities are built where crocodiles live, and people kill them because they are afraid of them and because their skins are worth a lot of money. People are now trying to protect them and their numbers are increasing, although some kinds of crocodile may still disappear forever.

Crocodiles are also grown on 'farms' for their meat and skins. This keeps some species alive – but they are not living in the wild.

a crocodile-skin handbag

a crocodile farm

Crocodile babies

Female crocodiles lay their eggs on a sandy bank near the water and they stay near their eggs to keep them safe until they **hatch**. This takes about 90 days.

When the baby crocodiles are ready to hatch out of the eggs, they make a squeaky sound to warn their mother to take care of them. They are now in great danger and many will be eaten by other animals, such as **monitor lizards**, before she can carry them safely to the water.

Monitor lizards

Monitor lizards look a bit like crocodiles but they are not related.
The largest monitor lizards in the world are the **Komodo dragons**.
They can grow up to three metres long and live for 20 to 40 years.

They like to hide and then rush at their prey and bite it with their powerful jaws. Their mouths contain poison and even if their prey escapes, it will often die later from blood poisoning. Crocodiles will sometimes attack humans, but Komodo dragons will hardly ever do so.

a forked tongue for sensing prey

Like crocodiles, monitor lizards are scavengers. They will eat anything they can find. They eat fish, dead animals, birds, frogs and other small animals. But they especially like eggs. They dig out crocodile eggs from the nest and eat them when the mother crocodile is away.

There are many different kinds of monitor lizard.
Some are as small as 25cm long.

good sense of smell

strong jaws

powerful tail

long, sharp claws

17

Monitor lizard babies

Baby monitor lizards have a special egg tooth which they use to chip their way out of their eggs. Crocodiles have one too. Mother crocodiles look after their baby hatchlings, but baby monitor lizards have to look after themselves.

Baby monitor lizards often live in trees where they are safe from adult lizards who might eat them. But like crocodiles, once they become adults, they are clever predators and scavengers, which is why these creatures have survived since the time of the dinosaurs.

Glossary

alligator   a relative of the crocodile that lives in North and South America

hatch   break out of an egg

Komodo dragons   a kind of monitor lizard

monitor lizards   lizards that look like crocodiles but are not related to them

Nile crocodiles   a kind of crocodile, named after a big river in Africa

prey   animals hunted for food by meat-eaters like crocodiles

saltwater crocodile   the largest type of crocodile in the world, able to live in both fresh water and seawater

scavengers   animals which eat food left by other animals or by people

Index

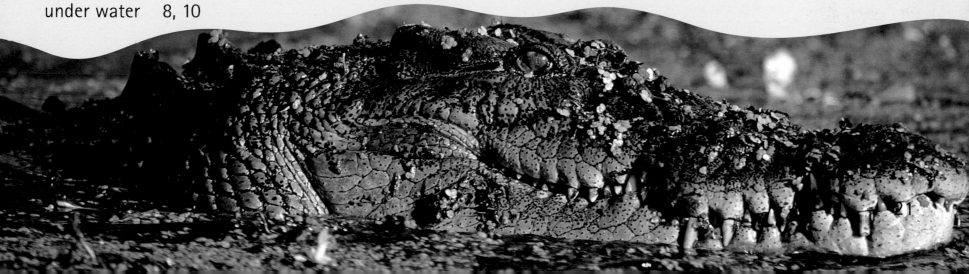

21

Fact chart

Crocodiles
live up to 80 years
up to seven metres long
have an egg tooth for chipping out of the egg
eat meat
eyes on top of their heads
powerful jaws and sharp teeth
look after their babies
powerful tail

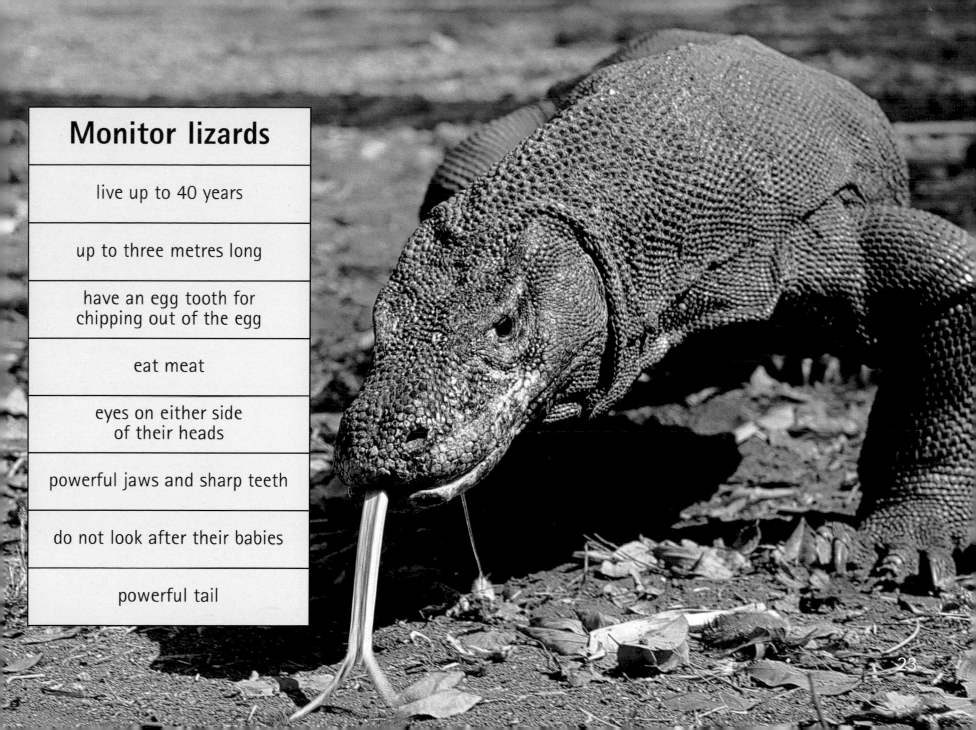

Monitor lizards

live up to 40 years

up to three metres long

have an egg tooth for
chipping out of the egg

eat meat

eyes on either side
of their heads

powerful jaws and sharp teeth

do not look after their babies

powerful tail

☙ Ideas for guided reading ☙

Learning objectives: adopt appropriate roles in small or large groups and consider ways of recording information; read and spell less common graphemes including trigraphs; draw together information and ideas from across the whole text, using simple signposts; explain their reactions to texts, commenting on important aspects

Curriculum links: Science: Humans and other animals

Interest words: alligator, egg tooth, Komodo dragon, monitor lizards, Nile crocodile, prey

Resources: whiteboard

Word count: 637

Getting started

- Ask the children to read the covers independently and leaf through the book deciding what kind of book this is and what it might tell us.
- Demonstrate reading pp2–3, and discuss what dinosaurs are.

- Encourage the children to describe the crocodile from the pictures (*e.g rough skin, sharp teeth*).
- Return to the contents page, and give each child a chapter to read independently, reminding them that they will be reporting back to the group on what they have found out.

Reading and responding

- Listen to each child read in turn as others read silently. Prompt and praise use of phonic strategies to decode unfamiliar words, as well as use of the glossary.
- Remind the children to use context to work out the meaning of any unfamiliar words they might meet.

Returning to the book

- Ask the children in turn to explain what they have researched, in their own words using the pictures to help them.
- Turn to pp22–23 and help the children to make up a quiz using facts e.g. *I live for 40 years, what am I?* Children try to be the first to answer.